Battle in the Air

By Rupert Matthews

Penguin
Random
House

LONDON, NEW YORK,
MELBOURNE, MUNICH, and DELHI

DK LONDON
Series Editor Deborah Lock
Editor Caryn Jenner
Senior Art Editor Ann Cannings
US Senior Editor Shannon Beatty
Producer, Pre-production Francesca Wardell

Reading Consultant
Dr. Linda Gambrell, Ph.D.

Subject Consultant
Ross Mahoney, Aviation Historian
RAF Museum, London

DK DELHI
Editor Pomona Zaheer
Art Editor Yamini Panwar
DTP Designers Anita Yadav, Vijay Kandwal
Picture Researcher Deepak Negi
Managing Editor Soma B. Chowdhury
Managing Art Editor Ahlawat Gunjan

First American Edition, 2015

Published in the United States by
DK Publishing
345 Hudson Street, 4th Floor
New York, New York 10014

15 16 17 18 19 10 9 8 7 6 5 4 3 2 1

001—270702—January/15

DK books are available at special discounts when purchased in bulk for sales promotions, premiums, fund-raising, or educational use
details, contact: DK Publishing Special Markets, 345 Hudson Street, 4th Floor, New York, New York 10014 or SpecialSales@dk.c

The publisher would like to thank the following for their kind permission to reproduce their photographs:
(Key: a-above; b-below/bottom; c-center; f-far; l-left; r-right; t-top)
1 Alamy Images: MasPix. 6 Dorling Kindersley: RAF Battle of Britain Memorial Flight (t). 11 Dorling Kindersley: Andy Crawford/By kind
permission of The Trustees of the Imperial War Museum, London. 12–13 Getty Images: Richard Bonson. 13 Getty Images: Fox Photos/Stringe
Hulton Archive (t). 15 Getty Images: Planet News Archive / SSPL (t). 16–17 Alamy Images: Juice Images (b). 18 Robert Harding Picture Libr
Tim Graham (t). 19 Corbis: Stefanie Grewel (b). 20 Getty Images: Imperial War Museums (b). 20–21 Dorling Kindersley: Rough Guides. 22 Do
Kindersley: RAF Battle of Britain Memorial Flight (t). 26 Alamy Images: phloen (b). 31 Alamy Images: nobleIMAGES (b). 32 Alamy Image
imageBROKER (b). 36 Dorling Kindersley: RAF Battle of Britain Memorial Flight (t). 38 Dreamstime.com: Luminis (b). 40 Getty Images: Popperfo
42 Corbis: Epoxydude/fstop (b). 43 Courtesy of the Royal Air Force Museum London: (t). 44 Alamy Images: A Amsel (t); Peter Wheeler (b
44–45 Dreamstime.com: Archipoch. 45 Alamy Images: Peter Wheeler (t); Corbis: Peter Cook/VIEW (b). 48 Getty Images: De Agostini Pictu
Library (b). 50 Dorling Kindersley: RAF Battle of Britain Memorial Flight (t). 53 Alamy Images: war posters (b). 54 Getty Images: Royal Air F
Museum/Hulton Archive (br). 54–55 Dreamstime.com: Jakub Krechowicz. 55 Alamy Images: Heritage Image Partnership Ltd (tl). 56–57 Dreams
com: Pictac. 57 Alamy Images: war posters. 58–59 Dreamstime.com: Albo. 60–61 Getty Images: Topical Press Agency / Hulton Archive. 62–63 C
Mark Stevenson/Stocktrek Images. 64 Corbis: Hulton-Deutsch Collection. 66–67 Dorling Kindersley: RAF Battle of Britain Memorial Flight (l
67 Dorling Kindersley: RAF Battle of Britain Memorial Flight (t, c). 68 Dorling Kindersley: Yorkshire Air Museum (c). 69 Courtesy of the Ro
Air Force Museum London: (b); Dorling Kindersley: Flugausstellung (c). 70 Dorling Kindersley: RAF Battle of Britain Memorial Flight (t). 73 C
Images: Planet News Archive/SSPL (b). 74 Corbis: Hulton-Deutsch Collection (t). 76–77 Dreamstime.com: Mark Sykes. 77 Getty Images: Li
Sheridan/Hulton Royals Collection (b). 81 Getty Images: Fred Morley/Hulton Archive. 82 Getty Images: Peter Dazeley/Photographer's Choice Rl
83 Getty Images: John Parrot/Stocktrek Images. 88 Dorling Kindersley: RAF Battle of Britain Memorial Flight (t). 91 Alamy Images: Detail
Heritage (b). 92–93 Getty Images: John Florea/Time Life Pictures. 94–95 Getty Images: Hulton Archive. 96–97 Getty Images: Planet News Arc
SSPL. 102–103 Dreamstime.com: Pitchayarat2514. 106 Getty Images: Harry Todd/Hulton Archive (t). 106 Dorling Kindersley: RAF Battle of E
Memorial Flight (b). 108 Dreamstime.com: Cristicotea (b). 110–111 Corbis: Trinette Reed/Blend Images. 113 Dreamstime.com: Sharpshot (b
114–115 Corbis: Mark Stevenson/Stocktrek Images. 116 Getty Images: Andrew Howe / E+ (b). 117 Corbis: Imperial War Museums (t
118–119 Dreamstime.com: Iva Villi. 120 Battle of Britain Memorial Trust: Malcolm Triggs. 121 Battle of Britain Memorial Trust: Barry Duff
122–123 Getty Images: Imagewerks/Imagewerks Japan. 122 Dorling Kindersley: RAF Battle of Britain
Memorial Flight (b). 123 Dorling Kindersley: RAF Battle of Britain Memorial Flight (b)
Jacket images: Front: Corbis: Mark Stevenson/Stocktrek Images; Back: Dorling Kindersley: RAF Battle of Britain Memorial Flight (tl, c)
Getty Images: Imagewerks/Imagewerks Japan (t); Spine: Corbis: Mark Stevenson/Stocktrek Images (b)
Endpapers: Dorling Kindersley: RAF Battle of Britain Memorial Flight

All other images © Dorling Kindersley
For further information see: www.dkimages.com

Discover more at
www.dk.com

Contents

This story is based on real events. All characters, places, and the RAF base and squadron named in the story are fictional.

The Battle of Britain, World War II

When: July 10th–October 31st, 1940

Where: The Battle of Britain was fought in the skies over southeast England between the British Royal Air Force (RAF) and the German Luftwaffe.

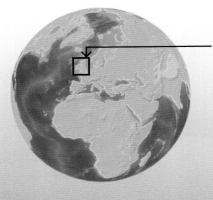

Great Britain

The white cliffs of Dover are a famous natural landmark on the coast of Kent in southeast England.

Great Britain is separated from the rest of western Europe by the English Channel.

N
W ← → E
S

Scotland

Northern Ireland

Ireland

England

Wales

London

Kent

Sussex   Dover

Brighton

● major cities in southeast England
Kent and Sussex are counties in southeast England

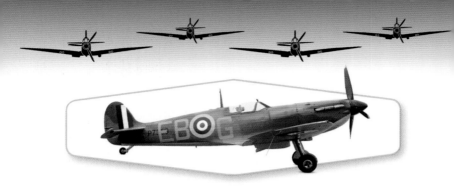

CHAPTER 1

Packing Up

Zoe put yet another book into the large cardboard box. It was nearly full. She gave a heavy sigh.

"But Grandma," she said. "I still don't understand why you need to move."

Zoe's grandmother was wrapping a china jug in bubble wrap. "We'll still be nearby. It's not as if your grandpa and I are moving away from England," she said. "We're not young any more, you know. Grandpa will be 92 at his next birthday."

"I know," said Zoe. "But what does Grandpa's birthday have to do with you moving? You love this old house."

"Come here, Zoe. Have a look at this brochure about our new apartment."

Zoe sat down next to Grandma and looked at the colorful booklet that she held out.

"There are lots of apartments designed for older people," Grandma continued. "It's close to the stores and there's even someone to help us with little jobs around the house. It'll be perfect for us."

"Zoe! Come and look at this!" It was the voice of Zoe's twin brother, Zak.

Zoe gave her grandmother's hand a quick squeeze, then hurried to the bedroom where Zak was sitting on the bed with Grandpa. They were looking at a battered old metal box.

"Look what we found!" said Zak.

"What is it?" asked Zoe.

"It's my old RAF locker," replied Grandpa. He rubbed his fingers over the top of the box.

"See this engraving?" he asked.

Zoe looked closely and saw the picture of an eagle with outstretched wings and the letters "RAF".

"What's RAF?" she asked.

"Royal Air Force," replied Grandpa. "I told you I was in the air force when I was younger."

Zak was getting impatient. "Can we open it?" he asked.

"Of course," said Grandpa. He pushed a button on the box and it sprang open. Inside, the children could see lots of photographs, pieces of paper, and some booklets. Grandpa pulled out a book with a leather binding. "Look, this is my old Flying Log Book with details of every time I flew. And here's my cap."

"You mean when you flew airplanes in World War II?" asked Zak.

Grandpa nodded. "That's right. I flew a Spitfire."

Zoe opened the book and read, "Flying Log Book. Pilot Officer George William Buckden. 1939." She turned to her grandfather. "What's a Pilot Officer?"

Grandpa smiled. "That takes me back. When I first joined the RAF, I had the rank of Pilot Officer, but later I was promoted to Flight Lieutenant. That was the rank I had during the Battle of Britain."

"Battle of Britain?" Zak echoed. "Wow, that sounds exciting!"

Grandpa stood up and went to look out of the window. "It was a long time ago," he said quietly. "They were terrible days. I even watched friends die. But we all worked together to help each other." He paused and wiped a tear from one eye. "Let's see what else is in the box."

Grandpa sat down again and pulled out a photo of two men in uniforms. "Here's a picture of me and my friend Panesar from No.606 Squadron." He looked at the photo more closely. "This picture was taken outside The Ugly Duck pub near RAF Lyddenstone. That's where I was based."

"What did you do there?" asked Zoe.

"Well," Grandpa replied, "German bombers used to fly over from France to attack England. The bombs killed lots of people and destroyed buildings. It was the job of my squadron to go up and fight the Germans in the air."

"Why were German aircraft in France?" asked Zak.

"The Germans had conquered France by then." Grandpa pulled an old newspaper page out of the box. "This is a report from September 3rd, 1939, the day the Second World War broke out. It's a speech by Neville Chamberlain, the British Prime Minister."

SAUSAGES GO BETTER WITH H-P SAUCE

Daily Herald

MONDAY, SEPTEMBER 4, 1939   ONE PENNY

No. 7349

ON YOUR FEET FOR HOURS? Than Don't Forget That
ZAM-BUK

WAR DECLARED BY BRITAIN AND FRANCE

The Fleet Moves Into Position

GREAT BRITAIN DECLARED WAR ON GERMANY AT 11 O'CLOCK YESTERDAY MORNING.

Six hours later, at 5 p.m., France declared war.

Britain's resolution to defend Poland against Nazi aggression was described by the newly-formed Ministry of Information in one of its first announcements, as follows:—

Navy Fully Mobilised

WAR CABINET OF NINE

Churchill Is Now First Lord

Unthinkable We Should Refuse The Challenge

—THE KING

POLES SMASH WAY INTO E. PRUSSIA

OFFICIALS in Warsaw stated late last night that the Polish army has smashed a way across the Northern border into East Prussia, after driving the Germans from several Polish towns in bitter fighting.

London Hears Its First Raid Warning

BLACK-OUT TIME TO-NIGHT—7.10.

BREMEN REPORTED TAKEN

MODERN CONCRETE CONSTRUCTION

CIVILIANS

Neville Chamberlain's Declaration of War

On September 1, 1939, German armies invaded Poland. Britain had promised to help Poland if that country were to be attacked. On September 3, British Prime Minister Neville Chamberlain broadcast a message on BBC Radio.

He said:

"This morning the British Ambassador in Berlin handed the German Government a final note stating that, unless we heard from them by 11 o'clock that they were prepared at once to withdraw their troops from Poland, a state of war would exist between us."

"I have to tell you now that no such undertaking has been received, and that consequently this country is at war with Germany."

Chamberlain's speech came as a blow to the British people, although they were well aware that war was likely. Older generations had already lived through World War I (1914–18) and they didn't want the country to endure another. However, most people agreed that war was necessary to stop the German forces from taking over Britain as well.

Grandma came into the room. "What's going on?" she asked. "We've got to be packed and ready to move by tomorrow."

"Just having a look at my old RAF box, darling," replied Grandpa.

"Let's take that with us to the new apartment," said Grandma. "There are a lot of memories in that old box."

"Were you in the RAF too, Grandma?" asked Zoe.

"Oh, goodness me, no," replied Grandma. "I was too young. I was in high school. But we still took part in the war effort. The school sports fields became gardens where we grew fruit and vegetables. 'Dig for Victory!' That was the slogan. We raised pigs, too. We had to do our part to make sure the country didn't run out of food, you see."

"What was it like going to school with a war going on?" asked Zak.

Grandma took Grandpa's hand.

"I used to look out of the classroom window and see aircraft fighting in the sky overhead," she told them. "I sometimes wonder if your grandpa was in one of those planes. I'm so grateful he's one of the lucky ones who survived."

Zoe and Zak looked at each other. They were grateful, too.

By the end of the afternoon, all of Grandma and Grandpa's things from the big house were packed up. Their new home was too small to fit everything, so there were boxes for the consignment shop, boxes for the garbage, and boxes for the kids to take home.

Zoe and Zak were quiet as they walked home from their grandparents' big old house for the last time.

Suddenly, Zak noticed a smile spread across his sister's face.

"I know that look," he said. "You've got an idea, haven't you?"

"Yup," said Zoe. "And it's going to make Grandma and Grandpa really happy."

Bayview Residential House

You will get a warm welcome from the staff and residents at Bayview House. We offer comfortable, independent living with full support services at a reasonable price.

BAYVIEW HOUSE was built in 1893 to be the home of Lord Stanley Polsted. Today it has been converted to contain 34 individual apartments together with a lounge, dining room, rec room, garden, and other features shared by all residents.

YOUR HOME will provide both privacy and comfort. It will contain a bedroom, kitchen, living room, bathroom, and small guest room/storage room. You can use the shared rooms, gardens, and facilities whenever you wish.

The local supermarket will deliver your groceries right to your front door. The caretaker can even help you order your groceries online, if you would like. The local restaurants will also deliver to your door.

Bayview has a caretaker living on the site who is available to help you with household tasks, such as changing light bulbs, moving heavy objects, or even opening jars!

The lovely beach town of Whitstable is a five-minute drive away, with a variety of amenities. A local taxi service is available at a reasonable price. We look forward to welcoming you to Bayview House.

MECHANICS AND ENGINEERS

THE ROYAL AIR FORCE is looking for men aged 18 to 42 who are experienced in engineering or mechanics. You must have good levels of fitness, possess good eyesight, and have no disabilities. A physical fitness test will be carried out before you are accepted.

We are seeking men who have:

✓ worked in a garage, or

✓ worked in a bicycle repair shop, or

✓ repaired industrial machinery.

Men who work on the railroads or on farms will not be accepted. Your jobs are already valuable to the war effort.

WANTED

If you volunteer now, you will:

- be trained to master craftsman level
- gain experience working on aircraft and on aircraft engines
- gain valuable experience that will help you get a good job when the war is over
- have the opportunity to train to be a pilot, air gunner, or navigator
- have the opportunity to work for promotion within the RAF

Remember—The Royal Air Force is one of the world's leading air organizations. Founded in 1918, the RAF is the oldest air force in the world. Men trained by the RAF are sought after by civilian air transportation companies in countries such as Canada, the USA, South Africa, India, and others around the world.

Volunteer to be a **Royal Air Force Engineer** NOW!

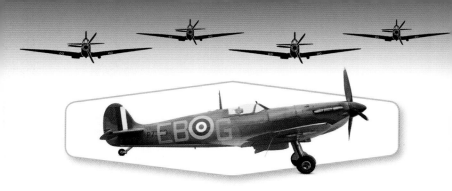

CHAPTER 2
Reunion Plans

"Did you see the look on Grandpa's face when he was talking about being in the RAF?" Zoe asked her brother.

Zak nodded. "He's sure got a lot of memories from the war."

"So let's organize a reunion for Grandpa and his old air force buddies!" she said. "We'll invite some of Grandma's friends from her old school, too."

Zak thought about Zoe's idea. "But how will we find these people?" he asked. "It was a long time ago."

"I know," said Zoe, "but Grandpa said he was in No.606 Squadron at RAF

Lyddenstone. We'll see if we can find some information on the Internet."

As soon as they got home, they asked their dad if they could use the computer.

"We've got research to do," said Zoe.

"What for?" asked Dad. "Are you working on a school project?"

The twins explained their plan for a wartime reunion.

"That's a sweet idea," he said. "But places might have changed, people might have moved away or even died. This might be an impossible task."

"But we've got to try," said Zak.

"Imagine how happy it would make Grandpa and Grandma," said Zoe.

"You're right about that," Dad agreed. "Okay, why don't you write a list of what you want to do and how to go about it? Then we'll discuss it."

Between them, the twins had lots of ideas. They made a mind map.

Reunion Mind Map

Research No.606 Squadron and the RAF base at Lyddenstone

• We know that No.606 Squadron no longer exists, but is RAF Lyddenstone still there?

• How can we contact people who served in the Battle of Britain with Grandpa?

• What do they remember about the Battle of Britain?

• Can they come to the reunion to meet Grandpa?

Research Grandma's old school

• What is it called?

• Does it still exist?

• Does the school keep records back to 1940?

• Can they help us contact Grandma's old school friends?

• What do Grandma's school friends remember?

• Can they come to the reunion to meet Grandma?

Find out more about World War II
and especially the Battle of Britain

- Who fought in World War II?
- Why did they fight?
- When was the Battle of Britain?
- Where did it take place?
- How was the battle fought?
- Why is the Battle of Britain important?

Things to do

Arrange the reunion for Grandpa
and Grandma to meet old friends

- Decide on a date and place for the reunion.
- Invite people to attend.
- Arrange food and drinks.
- Go to the reunion and make sure it all goes OK.

25

"Excellent," Dad remarked when they showed him their plans. He rubbed his chin. "In fact, there's something I can help with right away."

Rummaging in one of the boxes from Grandma and Grandpa's old house, he pulled out an old book.

"You need to know the name of Grandma's old school, don't you?" Dad opened the book. Inside was an inscription. "There's your answer," he told them.

Oxmore Girls School

To Violet Butterfield,
1st Prize in the
Oxmore Girls School
spelling competition

Zoe wrote "Oxmore Girls School" on their plan.

"Brilliant," said Zak. "Now we're going to start researching these places on the Internet. Okay, Dad?"

Dad smiled. "Okay."

The twins raced upstairs to the computer. First Zoe searched for Oxmore Girls School. They found the school website quite easily and jotted down the name of the headmistress and the address. The school was in the nearby county of Sussex, England.

Now it was Zak's turn. He typed "RAF Lyddenstone" into the search engine. What came up were some old pictures that looked like Grandpa's photo, but no recent information.

"I don't get it," he said. "It's as if RAF Lyddenstone disappeared."

"Look," said Zoe, pointing to an entry on the computer screen, "there's a village called Lyddenstone right here in Kent. That must be where the RAF base is. Let's ask Dad if he'll drive us there."

Dad agreed and the twins left a note for Mom when she got home from work.

Dear Mom,

Gone for a drive with Dad.

See you later.

Love,

Zak and Zoe

Twenty minutes later, they were peering out of the car windows as their father drove through the village of Lyddenstone.

"There's a church," said Zoe.

"And a duck pond," said Zak.

"And a pub called The Ugly Duck!" shouted Zoe, pointing to an old building with hanging baskets of flowers and some tables in front of it. A big picture of a duck dangled from a wooden beam. "Just like the pub in Grandpa's photo!"

Dad pulled the car to a halt and all three climbed out onto the sidewalk. On one side of the pub was a parking lot and on the other side was the entrance to an apartment complex. But there was no sign of an air base.

"Let's ask in the pub," said Dad.

He pushed open the big wooden door and went in. The twins followed. The room was warm and inviting, and several people sat at tables, eating and drinking.

"Can I help you?" asked the man behind the bar.

"I hope so," said Dad. "My father used to be based at RAF Lyddenstone. Do you know where it is?"

"That old RAF base is long gone," replied the bartender. "The runway was too short for modern aircraft and they couldn't extend it because the river's in the way. So the RAF sold the land to a developer who built those." He pointed outside to the apartment complex.

The twins sighed with disappointment.

"Well," said Dad, "how about going home and doing some research into the Battle of Britain?"

"If you're interested in the Battle of Britain, then you should see the nearby memorial," said the bartender.

The children perked up as Dad wrote down the directions. They drove to the coast, where tall, white cliffs overlooked the English Channel.

Zak read aloud from a plaque at the entrance. "'Never in the field of human conflict was so much owed by so many to so few.'"

"Winston Churchill said that. He was Prime Minister then." Dad was quiet for a moment. "It means we should all be grateful to people like Grandpa who fought for us in the Battle of Britain."

Up ahead they saw a large statue of a wartime pilot and two replica aircraft.

The children ran to have a closer look.

"This plane's a Hurricane," called Zak.

"This one's a Spitfire," said Zoe. "That's what Grandpa flew."

The children gazed at the statue of the pilot and tried to picture their lovable old Grandpa flying fighter planes. It was hard to imagine.

BRITAIN MEMORIAL · OPENED

On the way home, Zoe said, "Going to the memorial makes me want to have this reunion even more."

"Me too," Zak agreed. He opened the notebook that they'd brought with them. "Let's have a look at our plan."

The twins decided to write to the Royal Air Force Museum and to Oxmore Girls School. They debated whether to send emails or letters through the mail, and decided to send letters. As soon as they got home, they got to work.

Mom thought their plan for the wartime reunion for Grandma and Grandpa was great.

"They'll be thrilled if we can make the reunion happen!" she told the twins.

She helped them type their letters on the computer.

"We'll pop these in the mailbox tomorrow. Then all we've got to do is wait for the replies," said Zoe, as she stuck the stamps in the corners of the envelopes.

Zak groaned. "But I hate waiting!"

What does this quote mean?
"Never in the field of human conflict was so much owed by so many to so few."

Archives Division
Royal Air Force Museum, London
Grahame Park Way
London NW9 5LL

Dear Sir/Madam,

RE: Flight Lieutenant George William Buckden

We are writing to ask about any records you hold about our grandfather, Flt. Lt. George William Buckden, who served with No.606 Squadron during the Battle of Britain in 1940 and afterward.

We are particularly interested in contacting anyone still alive who served with our grandfather during the Battle of Britain. The reason for this is that we wish to reunite our grandfather with some of his old friends. We would be grateful if you could let us have contact details for any veterans of No.606 Squadron or RAF Lyddenstone from 1940.

Thank you for any help that you are able to give us.

Yours sincerely,

Zoe Buckden

Zoe Buckden

Zak Buckden

Zak Buckden

Miss Judith Vickers
Headmistress
Oxmore Girls School
School Lane, Oxmore
West Sussex
BN18 1LP

Dear Miss Vickers,

RE: Violet Butterfield

Our grandmother was a pupil at your school during the Battle of Britain in 1940. Her name was Violet Butterfield. She won the school spelling competition that year, which might help you to locate her in your files.

We are planning to hold a reunion of people that our grandparents knew during World War II. Would it be possible for you to give us contact details for any other pupils who were at Oxmore Girls School with our grandmother at that time?

Thank you for any help that you are able to give us.

Yours sincerely,

Zoe Buckden

Zoe Buckden

Zak Buckden

Zak Buckden

CHAPTER 3
About the War

Every day, Zak and Zoe rushed to the front door as soon as they heard the letters fall through the mail slot.

Meanwhile, the whole family helped Grandma and Grandpa settle into their new apartment. Zoe and Zak didn't like it nearly as much as their big old house, but it was cozy and Grandma and Grandpa seemed content there.

The children asked their grandparents more questions about their experiences in the war, but decided not to mention their plan for the reunion until they had some good news to report.

"How long will those replies take?" asked Zak on the third day. He flicked through the mail and handed it to his father with a disappointed sigh.

"I don't know," said Dad. "Give them a chance."

"There's plenty you can do in the meantime," said Mom. "What about continuing with your research into the Battle of Britain and World War II?"

"You can use the computer," Dad suggested, "and you also have the encyclopedia that Auntie Anne bought you last Christmas."

The twins raced up the stairs to the computer room.

"Winner gets to go first on the computer!" called Zak.

"I'm first," said Zoe, reaching the computer desk seconds before Zak. She searched for "Battle of Britain" on the Internet.

Zak turned the pages of the big encyclopedia to find "World War II".

He read aloud. "World War II lasted from 1939 to 1945. It was the largest war in history. Many countries around the world were involved, with the fighting nations divided into two groups, the Allies and the Axis."

WORLD WAR II

MAIN ALLIED POWERS
Australia, Canada, New Zealand, Russia (from June 1941), South Africa, United Kingdom (and the British Empire), United States (from December 1941)

MAIN AXIS POWERS
Germany, Italy, Japan

Key countries occupied by Germany:
Austria, Belgium, Czechoslovakia, Denmark, Estonia, France, Greece, Latvia, Lithuania, Netherlands, Norway, Poland, Yugoslavia

Zak took notes as he read. "Japanese leaders wanted to take over other countries in the Pacific. In Europe, the German dictator, Adolf Hitler, was also invading other countries. The war began in 1939, when Hitler invaded Poland. Britain and France were friends of Poland, so they declared war on Germany. Then Germany conquered France and other countries in Europe, but not Britain. In 1941, Russia and the United States joined the war on the Allied side."

"Here's the RAF Museum website," said Zoe. "They've got a whole exhibit about the Battle of Britain, with some real aircraft!"

"Maybe Mom and Dad will take us to the RAF Museum on Saturday," said Zak.

"Good idea!" Zoe agreed.

"The Germans conquered France in June 1940," she continued. "With Britain only 20 miles across the English Channel from France, everyone thought they would invade us next."

"Look," Zak added, pointing to a picture he recognized.

"Remember Dad said that Churchill was Prime Minister in 1940? This is part of the speech he made then.

'… The Battle of France is over. I expect that the Battle of Britain is about to begin… Hitler knows that he will have to break us in this island or lose the war. If we can stand up to him, all Europe may be free…'"

Zoe read on and gasped. "The German Luftwaffe had about four times more aircraft than the RAF! Poor Grandpa."

"But Grandpa did survive and we not only won the Battle of Britain, but the Allies won the war," said Zak.

"I know." Zoe clicked on another website. "This is dreadful, worse than I thought. It says here that all together about 60 million people died in the war."

Zak was quiet. It made him feel strange to think about so many people dying.

On Saturday, the twins and their parents went to the RAF Museum in London. Zak and Zoe liked seeing the aircraft that Grandpa had told them about, especially the Spitfire and the Hurricane, and they found out lots of information for their research from the Battle of Britain exhibit and the film "Our Finest Hour."

Zak even asked at the information desk if the museum had received their letter about locating Grandpa's RAF buddies, but he was told that it was a different department and they would have to wait for a reply.

At last, a letter arrived saying "RAF Museum" across the postmark. Zoe tore the letter open and read it quickly.

"What does it say?" asked Zak impatiently.

⊙ ROYAL AIR FORCE museum

Dear Zak and Zoe,

Thank you very much for your inquiry about No.606 Squadron. We do have contact details for one former member of the Squadron who served during the Battle of Britain. We have forwarded your letter to him and asked him to reply to you directly if he is interested in getting in touch with your grandfather.

"That's really exciting!" said Mom.

"But it means even more waiting!" groaned Zak.

43

Our visit to the RAF Museum,

We saw this Spitfire right outside the RAF Museum.
Can you imagine it taking off and soaring into the sky?

This made us sad. It's what's left of a Hurricane
that crashed during the Battle of Britain.
I wonder what happened to the pilot?

by Zak and Zoe

The Junkers Stuka was the most feared of the German bombers. Not only was it very accurate, it also had a loud siren that made a terrible howling noise as it attacked.

Zoe took this picture as we left the museum. The massive hangars are full of aircraft, many of them from World War II.

Battle of Britain Timeline: 1940

In the summer of 1940, the German army prepared to invade Britain. First, the Luftwaffe tried to gain control of the skies in what became known as the Battle of Britain.

August 1st German plan to invade Britain is scheduled to take place in the middle of September.

June 22nd France surrenders. Germany takes over airfields in northern France.

August 13th "Adlertag," German for "Eagle Day," was the first day of mass German attacks on RAF bases.

July 9th Luftwaffe aircraft start attacks on British ships in the English Channel.

August 15th Over 1,000 German aircraft attack Britain—the heaviest of the air attacks during the Battle of Britain.

1940

August 18th Called "The Hardest Day" by the RAF with 63 aircraft destroyed and 54 damaged, though only 10 pilots are killed and 19 injured.

August 24th Germans begin a series of heavy attacks on RAF fighter bases.

August 25th RAF start using pilots with as little as 9 hours of experience on fighters.

August 26th RAF start using Polish, Czech, and French pilots.

September 6th Several RAF bases are temporarily out of action and some squadrons reduced to less than half strength.

September 7th German bombing attacks switch from RAF bases to London and other cities in what is known as the Blitz. Over the next few weeks, nearly 1 million buildings are destroyed and 20,000 people killed in London.

September 17th Hitler orders the invasion of Britain to be postponed. The invasion is later canceled as the Germans invade Russia instead.

Britain Under Attack

This map shows the RAF bases involved in the Battle of Britain and major locations hit by German bombs during the Blitz.

During the Battle of Britain (July 1940–October 1940), battles raged across British skies as the RAF defended its bases against the might of the German Luftwaffe.

When Hitler realized that the Germans couldn't defeat the RAF, he started bombing cities and industrial areas in what was called the Blitz. He wanted to force Britain to surrender. Although tens of thousands of people died in the Blitz (September 1940–May 1941), and cities and homes were destroyed, the British people didn't give up. Popular slogans helped to keep up British spirits.

"LET US GO FORWARD TOGETHER"

KEY FOR MAP
* Major air raids
⊗ British RAF fighter bases
■ Main British industrial areas

48

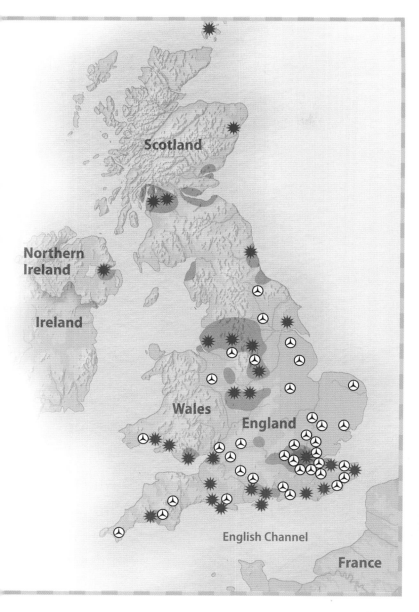

Scotland

Northern
Ireland

Ireland

Wales

England

English Channel

France

49

CHAPTER 4
Fighter Pilot

Three days later, the phone rang as the twins were doing their homework. Mom answered the phone, then looked puzzled.

"It's for you Zak," she said. "But it doesn't sound like one of your friends."

Zak took the phone. "Yes?" he asked. "Who?" Suddenly he grinned. "Wait, I've got to get my sister." He put the phone down. "Zoe, come here. Mom, how do you put on the speakerphone?"

Mom came over and pushed a button.

"Hello," came a voice over the loud speaker. It was a man's voice but it sounded uncertain.

"Hello," chorused the twins.

"Is that Zak and Zoe?" said the voice. "George Buckden's grandchildren?"

"Yes," said Zak.

"My name is Panesar Singh. I was a pilot in No.606 Squadron with your grandfather during the war."

"We know! Grandpa showed us your picture!" Zoe piped up excitedly.

"Did he?" Mr. Singh laughed. "Well, I received a call from the RAF Museum saying that you're trying to contact people from the squadron. I remember my friend, Buckden. I hope he's well?"

Zak and Zoe said that their Grandpa was indeed well. They explained their plans for a wartime reunion. Panesar Singh asked a few questions, but mostly he listened.

"So do you think you can come to the reunion?" asked Zoe.

"Well, I don't know about coming to Kent," said Mr. Singh. "I live in a retirement home in Whitechapel, East London. I'm in a wheelchair now. Perhaps you two could come here if your parents agree?"

"Mom, what do you think?" whispered Zak. "Can we go?"

Mom nodded and went to the phone to make the arrangements.

"Splendid," said Mr. Singh when they were done. "In the meantime, should I photocopy some pages from my memory book for your research?"

"Yes, please!" said the twins together.

A few days later, the pages from Panesar Singh's memory book arrived. The twins read them aloud to Dad at the kitchen table.

"Things don't change much, do they?" Dad remarked. "This man's uncle fought in Afghanistan. Our army went back

there again nearly a hundred years later."

"Mr. Singh says that when something went wrong on an airplane, the pilots would blame it on imaginary gremlins," said Zoe. "They sound like some kind of ghost or something."

Zak's eyes grew wide. "Awesome! I'd love to see a gremlin!"

"Not if it messed around with your plane," said Zoe. "You might crash."

Ask someone you know to write their memories in a memory book. It's a good way to find out about people's lives and experiences.

Mr. Singh's Memories

I was born in Bathinda in the Punjab, northern India, in 1918. At that time, the Punjab was ruled by Britain.

When I was a child, my Uncle Sodhi fought in the invasion of Afghanistan. He brought me a lovely Afghan scarf. I still have it and wear it on cold days.

I asked Uncle Sodhi if I could join his regiment, but he told me I should learn to fly. He said that aircraft were "the cavalry of the clouds." He and Father borrowed money to buy me flying lessons.

I went to Britain, and in 1938, I joined the Royal Air Force and learned to fly a Spitfire. I joined No.606 Squadron at RAF Lyddenstone. On September 5th, I shot down the first of many German bombers. I also flew many patrols. Later, I escorted British bombers on raids to Europe. The gremlins caused some trouble, but luckily I never saw one. In 1943, the RAF asked me to train new pilots.

After the war, I flew passenger aircraft for the British Overseas Airways Corporation (BOAC). In 1953, I trained to fly jet aircraft. That was exciting! I flew the route to Delhi, where I met a girl I had known at school. We were married and she came to England. We had two sons, two daughters, and 12 grandchildren. Every year, we visited our relatives in India, but I am too old for the journey now.

DELHI

Gremlins

Gremlins are about a foot tall. They look like little people, but with very big noses and thin legs. Gremlins enjoy tinkering with mechanical parts of aircraft, and love metal tools such as wrenches and screwdrivers. They steal tools, or hide them so that their human owners cannot find them. Gremlins will climb inside aircraft to fiddle with bits and pieces. This means that aircraft sometimes have problems when flying. It is the work of the gremlins.

Gremlins hitch rides on RAF aircraft all over the world. They climb on board an aircraft when nobody is looking, then fly around to different RAF bases where they set up new homes.

During World War II, gremlins caused lots of trouble for RAF crews. They would cause aircraft to malfunction just as they started out on a mission, or even over Germany. Some pilots and gunners said that they saw gremlins sitting on engines or walking along wings.

Some people think that gremlin damage was caused by careless mechanics. They say that people who saw the gremlins were suffering hallucinations caused by a lack of oxygen at high altitudes.

What do you think?

Whitechapel was in a different part of London than the RAF Museum, and this time Mom took the twins on the train. When they arrived at the retirement home, they were shown to a comfortable lounge where Panesar Singh waited in his wheelchair.

"Thank you for seeing us, Mr. Singh," said Zoe.

"Nonsense," he chuckled. "It's nice to have visitors. Now, what can I tell you?"

"Well, what do you remember about RAF Lyddenstone and No.606 Squadron?" asked Zak.

Mr. Singh rubbed his chin. "Yes, well. That was a long time ago. Let me see now. I remember that 1940 was an absolutely glorious summer."

"We had week after week of blazing sunshine. They talk about global warming these days, but summers now are nothing like that summer. It was lovely—worst luck!"

"What's wrong with sunny weather?" asked Zoe.

"Well, it helped the Germans, see," replied Mr. Singh. "They wanted to have clear skies so that they could spot the bomb targets clearly. We wanted stormy skies and rain clouds. That would have kept the Germans on the ground. Also, the Germans needed calm seas to get their army across the English Channel. The army never came, of course. They called off the invasion after we shot down so many of their aircraft."

"We were always tired. The Germans could come at any time from dawn to dusk. Our batman—an assistant guy— woke us before dawn with a cup of tea. Some pilots went straight to Dispersal in case the Germans came early, even in their pajamas, if it was warm. Or we had breakfast, then went to Dispersal."

"What's Dispersal?" interrupted Zak.

"That's where the Spitfires were, dispersed around the edge of the airfield," explained Mr. Singh.

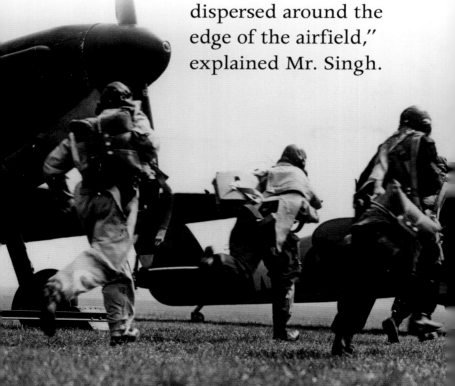

"If the aircraft were all parked together they'd be a good target for German bombers. While we waited, we played cards or read a book. If we heard the scramble bell, we had to jump into our aircraft and take off as fast as possible."

"When the radar detected German aircraft—radar was top secret then—our commander rang the bell to get us in the air. Then, as the Germans got over land, the Observer Corps watched them and phoned our headquarters saying where the German aircraft were. The headquarters then radioed us to tell us which direction to go."

"When we sighted the German aircraft, we tried to get above them. If possible we tried to get between them and the sun. That meant they had to look into the sun to see us. Then we attacked. We dived at the Germans, firing our guns. We zoomed past at top speed until we were out of range of their guns. Then the squadron leader gathered us together to see if anyone was missing and he'd decide if we should attack again."

"Sometimes the German fighters attacked us. Then there would be a dogfight. Each pilot would be twisting and turning, trying to shoot at the enemy without being shot at himself. It was terrible."

"Everything happened very fast. I saw several of my friends killed when their Spitfires were shot down. But we got a lot of Germans, too."

"Not everyone who was shot down was killed. Some men were wounded. We went to see our friends in the hospital when we could, but usually we were too busy. The Germans who came down by parachute were well taken care of. If they were wounded, they went to the hospital. If not, they were put in prison. They stayed in prison until the end of the war."

"Sometimes we had to fly out over the sea to attack the German bombers. If we were shot down there, we had a life jacket that would keep us afloat. Men in the bombers had rubber dinghies to keep them dry and homing pigeons that carried a message saying where the dinghy was so they could be rescued. But there was no space in a fighter for the dinghy and we didn't have a pigeon either. We had to hope another pilot saw us go down and radioed for a boat to come for us."

"If we weren't shot down, then we would land back at base. We had a few minutes' rest while the ground crew put new fuel and ammunition in our Spitfires. Then we were off again. Some days we had to scramble eight or ten times. On the few cloudy days, we were given some rest and slept in chairs near our Spitfires out on the airfield at Dispersal. When darkness came we went straight to bed. We were so tired all the time, that's what I remember."

Zoe and Zak were fascinated. "Thank you so much for talking to us, Mr. Singh," said Zak, as they said goodbye.

"I hope there's some way you can come to the reunion," Zoe added. "I'm sure Grandpa would love to see you!"

Panesar smiled. "Well, give old Buckden my regards."

Supermarine Spitfire

The most famous British fighter of World War II, the Spitfire was fast, turned easily, and was loved by its pilots. It had very modern features, but was expensive to make and needed lots of maintenance work to keep it flying. During the Battle of Britain, the Spitfire was used by 19 RAF squadrons.

SUPERMARINE SPITFIRE MKII, 1940

Origin	UK
Top speed	357 mph (575 km/h)
Bomb load	none
Number of guns	8

Aerial mast for high frequency (HF) radio

Rudder is fabric-covered

RAF roundel type A1 with wide yellow outer ring

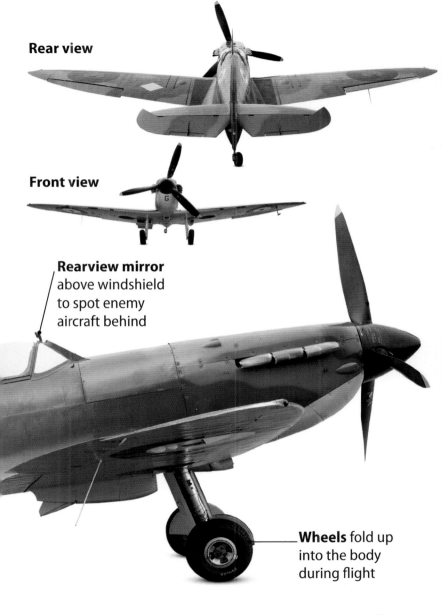

Rear view

Front view

Rearview mirror above windshield to spot enemy aircraft behind

Wheels fold up into the body during flight

67

Hawker Hurricane Mk I, 1936

The Hurricane was slower than the Spitfire, but just as heavily armed. It was considered a "good gun-platform," meaning

Origin	UK 
Top speed	328 mph (528 km/h)
Bomb load	none
Number of guns	8

that pilots hit their targets. It was also cheap to make and needed little maintenance. During the Battle of Britain, 39 RAF squadrons had the Hurricane.

Messerschmitt Bf109E, 1938

This was the most common German fighter in the Battle of Britain. It was similar to the Spitfire in speed and firepower.

Origin	Germany
Top speed	355 mph (572 km/h)
Bomb load	none
Number of guns	2 plus 2 cannon

However, it could fly only 375 miles without refueling. This restricted the time it spent in combat over Britain.

68

Heinkel He111, 1940

The Heinkel 111 was the main German bomber during the Battle of Britain. It was reliable and dropped bombs accurately.

Origin	Germany
Top speed	270 mph (434 km/h)
Bomb load	7,165 lbs (3,250 kg)
Number of guns	7

However, it was vulnerable to modern fighters and many were shot down during the Battle of Britain.

Junkers Ju87 Stuka

The Stuka divebomber was known to drop bombs with unusual accuracy. Some German Stuka pilots even said they could hit a target the size of a kitchen table every time. Its howling siren struck fear during the Battle of Britain.

Origin	Germany
Top speed	348 mph (547 km/h)
Bomb load	1,543 lbs (700 kg)
Number of guns	2

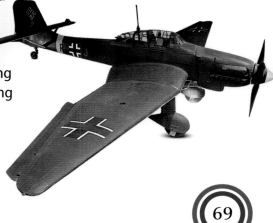

CHAPTER 5
Ack Ack

On Tuesday, Zak and Zoe received another letter.

"It's from someone called Doris Lilley who was at RAF Lyddenstone with Grandpa," said Zak once he'd pulled the letter out of the envelope. "She says she fired an ack ack gun, whatever that is. She's invited us for afternoon tea at the RAF Club in London."

"Very fancy," commented Dad. "We'll have to wear our best clothes."

A week later, they met Mrs. Lilley in the grand dining room of the RAF Club. She had silver hair and a lively smile. She shook hands with the children first and then with their parents.

"What's an ack ack gun?" blurted out Zak as soon as they sat down.

"An ack ack gun was an anti-aircraft gun," Mrs. Lilley answered. "The proper name was 'QF 3.7 inch' because it fired shells 3.7 inches across. That's about 10 centimeters, I think. Huge great thing, it was. Made an awful noise when we fired it."

"They allowed women to fire guns back then?" asked Zoe.

"Well, not at first," said Mrs. Lilley. "To start with, we carried ammunition, cleaned guns, and things like that. But later on, they needed the men to fight in the front line, so they trained us girls to do the shooting as well."

"It must have been exciting," said Zoe.

Mrs. Lilley took a sip of tea. "I suppose it was exciting," she said, "but not really very nice. We lived in a cold, drafty wooden hut next to the gun. It was about a mile from the Air Force buildings, even farther from any stores, and all we had was one bike between us. No hot water, unless we boiled it in the kettle—and that meant getting firewood for the stove. All a little miserable, really."

"So not swanky like this," said Zak, gesturing at the elegant surroundings of the RAF Club.

"I should say not!" Mrs. Lilley chuckled. "We lived with another gun crew and took turns to be on duty, day and night. When the air raid siren sounded, we raced outside to man the gun. It didn't matter what the weather was—rain, snow, wind, sun—we went and stood in the open to work the gun."

"We had to wear these heavy iron helmets—tin hats we called them. They stopped us from being killed or injured by the metal scraps from the shells and bullets that fell from the sky during a raid. Of course, if a bomb hit then that was it. And the Germans did try to bomb us, of course. They did not like us shooting at them one bit."

"So it was dangerous?" asked Zoe.

"Oh, yes," said Mrs. Lilley, "but not as dangerous as actually flying. I don't know how men like your grandfather did it. Going up to fight and be shot at, and so many of them were killed."

"Everyone had a dreadful time," Mrs. Lilley continued, "but the air base was not all about aircraft and guns. I think we had over five hundred people at RAF Lyddenstone altogether. There were many jobs to be done."

"Meals were served over at the main buildings. There were large kitchens with cooks and people to wash the dishes. Also, there were the girls who folded the parachutes for the pilots—a very important job—and aircraft maintenance crews, too. Their job was crucial."

"Then there was the hospital, of course. Not to mention all the clerks who did paperwork and administration like paying wages and checking that we had enough food and ammunition."

"Once I met the King of England after we shot down a German bomber," recalled Mrs. Lilley. "Part of me felt sad that I'd killed another human being. But then I thought if I hadn't shot him down, he could have killed a lot more of us." She was quiet for a moment. "Meeting the King was very exciting. They even let me use the bathroom to wash my hair specially!"

Captain Helen Smith
Your Majesty, may I introduce Corporal Lilley?
Corporal Lilley is the woman who shot down
a German bomber last week.

King George VI
Congratulations, Corporal Lilley.

Doris Lilley
Thank you, your Majesty.

King George VI
How did you manage to do it?

Doris Lilley
Well, I had a lot of help from my comrades.
I command the gun, but Gunner Lale aims it
and Gunner Barry loads. We heard the engines
of several aircraft flying toward London. Then
I saw a German bomber in a searchlight beam.

King George VI
This was at night?

Doris Lilley

Yes, that's right. About two o'clock in the morning.
I used the range finder to work out how far away
the bomber was and how high in the air it was.
I gave those figures to Gunner Lale. She worked
the controls to swing the gun around and aim it.
Then Gunner Barry loaded the gun and we fired.

King George VI

Who actually fires the gun?

Doris Lilley

Oh, I do. I am in command of the gun, you see.
So we fired, and we hit the bomber. I saw smoke
pour out of the aircraft. Then it began to dive. I saw
parachutes open as the German crew jumped out.

King George VI

Good job, Corporal Lilley.
You and your crew have
done splendid work.

The Royal Family 1940

Doris Lilley

Thank you, your Majesty.

The British Royal Family

Despite the dangers, King George VI
and Queen Elizabeth stayed in
London throughout the war.
Princesses Elizabeth and Margaret
were sent to nearby Windsor.

Mrs. Lilley smiled. "I remember Christmas 1940 at RAF Lyddenstone. It was my first Christmas away from home. I really missed my family, especially my mom, but I'd made friends with Mary Lale and Brenda Barry, the other girls in my gun crew. We shared a room in the hut near the ack ack gun."

"That Christmas, we made paper decorations for our room. We made presents for each other too, since there were no stores nearby. We didn't have much money in any case. I remember knitting Mary a pair of socks to wear in bed and Brenda gave me a handkerchief that she had embroidered herself."

"The meals at the mess hall were horrible in the few weeks before Christmas. We didn't know that the cooks were saving food for Christmas Day. Imagine our delight when they served up a scrumptious Christmas lunch of roast chicken with vegetables, followed by a real Christmas pudding. We were each given only a few spoonfuls of pudding, but it was very tasty."

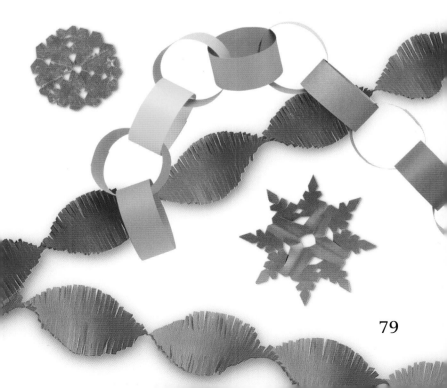

"That afternoon, we had to run out to man our gun since there were some German bombers nearby. After two hours in the freezing cold, we were finally allowed back indoors. Then Mary, Brenda, and I had a lovely cup of hot tea and shared the small Christmas cake that my mom had sent me."

Mrs. Lilley pointed to the cream cakes on the china dish. "My mom's cakes were even tastier than these. Our cooks at the base used to bake lovely cakes, too, despite the food shortages." She paused. "Anyway, what's all this about a reunion? It sounds a fantastic idea."

Zak and Zoe explained their plans while Mrs. Lilley jotted down notes. When they had finished, she put her notebook away and smiled. "I'll be there," she said.

Food Rationing

The German army tried to cut off the supply of goods to Britain from other countries, causing food shortages. In 1940, the government introduced rationing to ensure there was enough for everyone.

Ration books
When people paid for groceries, the shopkeeper signed their ration books or cut out the correct coupons.

Rationed foods
These are some of the foods that were rationed: chocolate and sweets, milk, meat, eggs, cheese, sugar, cooking fat, tea, and jam.

Ration posters

Posters explained the need for rationing. Without rationing, one person might buy up all of the food, leaving none for anyone else. Rationing meant everyone received at least a small share.

Thrifty Cooking

These recipes show cooks how to be resourceful. (In the 1940s, Great Britain used imperial measurements, although now they use the metric system.)

Tips for using up
STALE BREAD

FAIRY TOAST

Cut thin slices of bread and bake in a moderate oven until crisp and golden brown. Store in an airtight container. Use as a standby in place of bread or crackers. It will keep for months!

WHEATMEALIES

Half-dozen slices stale bread, ¼ in. thick

Cut into ¼-in. squares. Put on a baking sheet and bake in the oven on low heat till brown and crisp. Store in a container. Serve with milk and sugar to taste.

Tips for using up
STALE BREAD

SUMMER PUDDING

8 oz. fresh fruit (red or purple, if possible) · *¼ pint water*
1-2 oz. sugar · *5 oz. stale bread, cut ¼-½ in. thick*

Stew the fruit with the sugar and water until soft.
Line a pint-size bowl with a round of bread at
the bottom and fingers of bread around the sides.
Fit the fingers of bread together so the bowl doesn't
show through. Half-fill the bowl with stewed fruit.

Cover the fruit with a layer of bread scraps. Add the
remaining fruit and cover with another layer of bread.

Pour the rest of the juice over the pudding and
cover it with a weighted plate or saucer.
Leave for at least two hours
to cool and set. Turn out
carefully and serve
with custard.

N.B.—Very juicy fruit does
not require any water for
stewing. Bottled fruit may be
used if fresh fruit is not available.

Mechanic's Instructions for Maintenance of the Spitfire Mk1a

The Mark 1a Spitfire is a very modern aircraft.
The work you do must be precise. Be very careful.

WORK TO BE DONE EVERY MORNING

REMEMBER THE SAFETY OF THE AIRCRAFT AND CREW IS YOUR RESPONSIBILITY!

• Check fuel tank is full.

• Check engine has enough oil.

• Check tires have correct air pressure.

• Check oxygen tank that pilot uses at high altitude. Replace if less than half-full.

• Ensure controls for flaps, ailerons, tail fin, and rudder work smoothly.

• Start engine and run it up to full revs for 1 minute. Listen for any unusual noises.

• Ask pilot for anything to report about the aircraft.

WORK TO BE DONE EVERY WEEK

• Remove and test spark plugs and carburetor.

• Test tension on the wires from controls to flaps, ailerons, tail fin, and rudder. Tighten as necessary.

• Move aircraft to gun test area. Test to make sure guns fire straight. Adjust as necessary.

• Inspect aircraft skin for dents, cuts, or other marks. Repair as necessary.

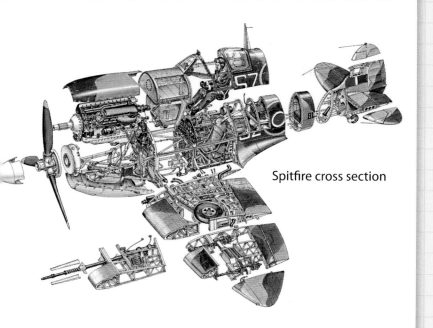

Spitfire cross section

WORK TO BE DONE EVERY MONTH OR AFTER 100 FLYING HOURS

• Remove engine from aircraft. Take engine apart and inspect all moving parts. Replace worn parts as necessary.

• Remove guns from aircraft. Take guns apart and inspect all moving parts. Replace worn parts as necessary. Clean insides of gun barrels.

• Check all controls, straps, and buckles in cockpit. Replace as necessary.

• Inspect wheels and legs. Check all moving parts. Replace worn parts as necessary.

CHAPTER 6

Dangerous Schooldays

A few days later, the children received a letter from Oxmore Girls School. Zoe tore it open and started reading.

"Well?" demanded Zak. "What does the letter say?"

"It's from the headmistress." Zoe scanned down the letter. "She says that two women who were pupils during the war are going to be visiting the school soon and she's invited us to meet them."

"Great!" Zak exclaimed. "I wonder if they were friends of Grandma's?"

The following Saturday, Mom drove
Zak and Zoe to Oxmore Girls School in
Sussex, where they were greeted by
a woman in a stylish suit.

"Hello, I'm Judith Vickers, the
headmistress," she said. She introduced
the two elderly ladies with her. "This
is Helen Probert and Margaret Naker."

"Do you remember our Grandma?"
Zak asked them. "She was called
Violet Butterfield before she married
our Grandpa."

"Oh, yes," smiled Helen Probert.
"A real handful, Vi was. Always
getting into trouble."

"Really?" gasped Zak. He couldn't
imagine his sweet old Grandma getting
into trouble!

"Let's just say that she always made us
laugh," chuckled Margaret Naker. "Give
Vi our best regards, will you?"

The children nodded.

"Can I show you around?" asked Miss Vickers. "The school has changed a lot since the war days, but there are a few things left from back then."

She led the way around the side of the school buildings.

Mrs. Probert took Zoe's arm for support. "I'm a little unsteady on these old legs of mine," she said.

"The big air raid shelter was here." Miss Vickers pointed to a patch of grass. "I believe it was made of concrete and sunk right down into the ground."

"That's right," chipped in Mrs. Naker. "I remember the concrete steps going down into the ground. A long way, too; over ten feet, I think."

"The top of the shelter was covered with dirt," added Mrs. Probert. "We used to play on it. Do you remember sliding down the snowy slope in the winter, Margaret?"

90

"But the air raid shelter's gone now," said Zak in disappointment.

"The next one isn't," said the headmistress. "This way. The gardener uses it to store tools now."

She led the way to a small structure tucked behind a modern sports hall. It looked like a garden shed made out of metal sheets.

"It's an Anderson shelter," said Mrs. Naker. "We had one in our backyard. My dad built it for us as soon as the war broke out."

"This shelter was the ARP center for the school," said Mrs. Probert.

"What's ARP?" asked Zoe.

"It means Air Raid Precautions. ARP protected people from the dangers of air raids," Mrs. Naker explained. "Every village and town had them and the people who volunteered to be ARP wardens made sure that everyone followed the instructions to the letter."

"Do you remember the blackouts at night?" asked Mrs. Probert. "They were awful. We couldn't show any lights in case a German bomber pilot saw them. You had to put thick black material over your windows so no light shone out."

"All the streetlights were off," Mrs. Naker added, "and you weren't allowed flashlights or anything. It was OK by moonlight, but on cloudy nights it was pitch black. You had to walk really slowly, feeling your way in the dark until

92

you reached where you were going." She turned to Mrs. Probert and laughed. "Remember that night Violet said she knew the way home in the dark and then fell in the pond?"

"What about car headlights?" asked Zak. "Couldn't you put those on?"

"Only doctors were allowed to use cars, and the army, of course," replied Mrs. Naker, "but not ordinary people. All the gas went to the war effort."

"If you had a car, you had to take the wheels off so that German invaders couldn't use it," put in Mrs. Probert.

Miss Vickers showed them inside the ARP center. "I believe the warden on duty sat in here."

"That's right," said Mrs. Naker. "He would get a phone call to tell him if the German bombers were coming, and then he'd sound the siren."

Why couldn't lights be on at night?
Who sounded the air raid siren?

"That siren was so loud you could hear it all over town!" Mrs. Probert exclaimed. "Whenever it sounded, we knew German aircraft were coming. We all took cover in the shelters, except the warden who stayed here. When the bombers were gone, he sounded the All Clear siren to tell people it was safe to come out."

Zak and Zoe listened to everything the women told them.

"Grandma said the sports fields were made into garden plots," said Zoe.

Mrs. Probert pointed to what was now a large soccer field. "They were over there," she said. "I loved growing the fruit and vegetables and thinking that I was contributing to the war effort. After I left school, I became a land girl and helped on a farm in the countryside."

"She also said you even raised pigs in the schoolyard," said Zoe.

"I'd forgotten about those!" Mrs. Naker laughed. "Helen, do you remember that pig with the black spot? He was always full of mischief."

"Just like your Grandma," Mrs. Probert told the children. "We can't wait to see her at this reunion!"

How could people help
the war effort?

Oxmore Girls School

Oxmore Girls School
School Lane
Oxmore
Sussex

June 14, 1940

Dear Parent,

You will be aware that the government revised the rules on food rationing last week.

The new rations for each girl are:

bacon and ham	4 ounces per week
sugar	8 ounces per week
butter	2 ounces per week
lard	2 ounces per week
meat	6 ounces per week

We expect there will be rations on eggs, jam, and sweets in the near future.

Other foods, such as flour and fruit, are not rationed, but they can sometimes be hard to find.

As soon as war was declared, we began growing vegetables and fruit in our gardens and two of our sports fields. We have now decided to dig up our last sports field and use it to grow food. In the future, we will be sharing a sports field with Oxmore Boys School.

In addition, our pig club will be expanded. From next month, we will be raising three pigs. Please send any food waste to school to be fed to our pigs. When a pig is slaughtered, half the meat will go to the government and half to our school. We will raffle half of our meat allocation to parents. Tickets will cost one shilling each.

Yours faithfully,

Mildred Glynleigh

Mildred Glynleigh
Headmistress

99

Oxmore Girls School

Air Raid Procedures

1. Obey instructions from teachers and class monitors at all times.

2. All girls must carry gas masks at all times. The gas mask box is to contain the gas mask only and is not to be used to carry any other items.

3. On hearing the air raid siren, girls will walk calmly to the nearer of the two air raid shelters. Running is not permitted.

4. If you should hear bombs exploding or guns firing, immediately lie down on your stomach. Place your hands over your head. Keep your eyes closed.

5. In case of injury, follow your first aid training. Walking wounded should report to the First Aid Station in the Staff Room. Teachers will attend those unable to walk and will administer first aid.

6. If you see a fire, sound the fire alarm immediately. Fire buckets and beaters are available at several locations in the school for dealing with minor fires.

7. When the "All Clear" sounds, assemble beside the main gates of the school. Do not go into the school until instructed to do so. There may be an unexploded bomb present.

Remember—The aim of the enemy is to cause panic. Keep calm at all times. Your courage will win us victory.

MONDAY SEPTEMBER 2, 1940

First day back at school after the summer vacation. The girls are very nervous. I have received letters from the parents of three girls saying that their daughters have been evacuated to other parts of the country to escape the bombing. I hope they find good schools at their new homes. They will need a good education.

TUESDAY SEPTEMBER 3, 1940

The war is one year old today. At lunchtime, we heard heavy explosions to the south. From the schoolyard, we could see anti-aircraft shells exploding and some aircraft. They must be German bombers. Madeleine Walders (Class 3B) twisted her ankle trying to climb a tree to get a better view of the bombing. Silly girl.

WEDNESDAY SEPTEMBER 4, 1940

The air raid sirens sounded at 11 o'clock last night. I went to our Anderson shelter with my neighbors, the Watsons. We heard loud explosions nearby. We learned later that a bomb had struck a chicken farm. At 10 o'clock this morning, the air raid siren sounded again. The girls all behaved well. A large number of enemy aircraft flew over heading north, but they dropped no bombs. The All Clear sounded at 11 o'clock.

THURSDAY SEPTEMBER 5, 1940

Another air raid and another night in the Anderson shelter. Mrs. Watson forgot her false teeth and ran back to their house. "Come back", shouted Mr. Watson. "It's bombs they're dropping, not pork pies". I had to laugh. Several girls were late to school today. There was an unexploded bomb in Lammas Lane. The lane was closed so they had to walk around the long way. The army sent a man who defused the bomb and made it safe. He must be very brave; the bomb could have gone off at any moment.

FRIDAY SEPTEMBER 6, 1940

During morning break, we heard a loud engine noise, followed by strange popping sounds. A large aircraft with two engines and huge black crosses on the wings flew low over the playground. A German bomber! Everyone lay flat on the ground. Then a smaller aircraft with round markings came chasing the German. It was a Hurricane firing its guns. They were out of sight within seconds. Nobody was hurt. We learned later that the bomber had crashed in a field near Birdham. All the German crew were killed.

Everyone can help the war effort—even children!

Dig for victory

Grow food to feed our country.

Make do and mend

Fabric is needed to make life-saving parachutes for the armed services, so mend your old clothes and adjust them to fit as you grow.

Knit for the forces

Use leftover wool to knit socks and scarves for our boys in the forces.

Save metal

Donate unwanted pots and pans and other household items. The metal can be melted down to make planes and ships.

How to help when you're older

Men aged 18-41 must enlist in the armed forces

Royal Air Force (RAF)
Royal Navy
Royal Marines
British Army
Merchant Navy

Women's forces

Women's Auxiliary Air Force (WAAF)
Women's Royal Naval Service (WREN)
Women's Auxiliary Territorial Service (ATS)

Air Raid Precautions (ARP) wardens

Sound air raid sirens and help people take cover in air raid shelters. Carry out first aid as necessary and help to put out fires. Enforce the blackout policy.

Home Guard

Men too young or too old for the armed forces are needed to protect Britain on the home front.

Women's Volunteer Services (WVS)

Help evacuate children to safer parts of the country and to feed and clothe refugees.

Women's Land Army

Help grow much-needed food while farmers are at war.

Factory workers, bus drivers, clerks, etc.

Women are needed to take over many jobs while men are at war.

CHAPTER 7

Reunion

Zoe and Zak worked hard to organize the reunion. With Mom and Dad's help, they arranged a lunch for everyone in the function room at a pub in the nearby town of Whitstable.

"Guess what? The North Kent Telegraph is going to send a photographer and reporter along," Zoe announced. "They seem really interested in the reunion."

"That's great!" Zak checked the guest list. "Mrs. Lilley the ack ack gunner is coming, so are Helen and Margaret, Grandma's two school friends, and

Miss Vickers, the current headmistress at Oxmore School. We also received an email from Great-uncle Tom. He's got memories of the war, too, so he wants to come. Only Panesar Singh can't make it."

You are invited

to a reunion lunch

in honor of those who served with George Buckden at RAF Lyddenstone

during the Battle of Britain and school friends of

Violet Buckden from Oxmore Girls School

WHERE

The Red Bull Inn, Whitstable, Kent

WHEN

June 15 at 12 noon

RSVP to Zak and Zoe Buckden

"That's a shame," said Mom.
"He sounded really excited to see your
Grandpa again. And I'm sure Grandpa
would like to see him."

"I know," Zak agreed, "but Mr. Singh
says it will be too difficult for him to
travel on the train on his own with
his wheelchair."

"Why don't you have a word with
the newspaper about Mr. Singh,"
said Dad. "They might help."

Zoe gave them a call. When she
got off the phone, she was smiling.

"The newspaper editor is so excited for Mr. Singh to be part of the reunion that they've offered to pay for a taxi to bring him from London."

"That's fantastic," said Dad.

Zoe nodded. "They'll also pay for the lunch and any other expenses if they can have an exclusive story about the reunion. So we've got to keep a record of all the money we spend for the reunion, along with the receipts."

"That's generous of them," said Mom.

"Grandma and Grandpa are really looking forward to the reunion, too," added Zak. "We went to visit them at their new apartment today. Grandma has that little sparkle in her eye and Grandpa said he's even writing a speech!"

"We did it!" Zoe gave her brother a high five.

He grinned. "I think we're all ready for the reunion!"

On the day of the reunion, Zak and Zoe and their mother arrived at the pub early.

"Everything's ready," said the pub landlord. "Here come the newspaper reporter and photographer."

"I want to get photos of everyone as they arrive," said the photographer.

Soon, Dad came in the car with Grandma and Grandpa, who were very excited. Then everyone else arrived and there were lots of hugs and handshakes and shrieks of "You haven't changed a bit," although more than 70 years had passed. Zak and Zoe looked at all the smiles in the room, and felt quite proud of all their hard work.

Once everyone was seated, Grandma tapped her glass with a spoon to make a ringing sound. The room fell silent.

"This is a very special reunion," she said, getting to her feet. "Zoe and Zak, you've really made us proud. It's so wonderful seeing my old school friends again after all these years. I was nearly evacuated in 1940, but then my dad decided I should stay at home and finish school. But my little brother Tom here was sent to stay with a family in Devon."

"Being away from home was awful," said Great-uncle Tom. "I missed my family and friends, and my mom's cooking!" he added, patting his tummy.

Everyone laughed.

"Anyway," continued Grandma, "I'll hand over to George now."

She sat down and Grandpa stood up. "First of all," he began, "a big thank you to Zak and Zoe. They've done a

112

wonderful job organizing this reunion.
I've particularly enjoyed seeing Panesar
again. In fact, if it were not for
him I would not be here."

POST CARD

FOR ADDRESS

ILFRACOMBE
1 –PM
9 SEP
1940
DEVON

FOR CORRESPONDENCE

Dear Vi,
How are you? Hope Oxmore
hasn't been hit too badly.
Devon is all right, I suppose,
but I really miss home,
especially Mom's cooking!
Take good care.
Love,
Tom

Miss Violet Butterfield
Rose Cottage
Park Street
Oxmore
Sussex

"It was a lovely, sunny day in September 1940 when we were told a large German bomber force was coming. We scrambled and flew out to find them. We went to attack, but didn't see a force of Messerschmitts flying escort high above. They came down on us like a pack of hounds. My instrument panel exploded as it was hit by machine gun bullets. I put the Spitfire into a spin, but one German stayed with me."

"More bullets hit my wings. Suddenly the German plane caught fire and dived away. Panesar flashed past, giving me a thumbs-up sign."

"He'd shot the Messerschmitt down and saved my life."

There was a round of applause.

"So thank you to Panesar, and thank you again to Zak and Zoe."

Grandpa waited until the applause died away. He lifted his glass of wine. "I'd like to propose a toast." Everyone raised their glasses. "To all our old comrades who are no longer here," said Grandpa, as a tear trickled down his cheek.

RAF Lyddenstone Heroes Reunite

Survivors of the Battle of Britain reunited this week. The veterans all served at RAF Lyddenstone in 1940. The meeting took place at the Red Bull in Whitstable on Saturday at lunchtime.

Present at the reunion were Spitfire pilots George Buckden and Panesar Singh, together with Doris Lilley, who manned an anti-aircraft gun at the air base. All three are aged over 90 years, but their memories remain clear.

"I remember so many of the men I fought with," said George Buckden. "Too many of them were killed during the war, but I'm glad to see Panesar again. He is a real hero."

Panesar Singh replied, "Everyone was a hero. We pilots got the glory, but everyone did their part. They were exciting times, but sad, too. What the world really needs is peace. War is a terrible thing."

RAF medals for bravery during World War II

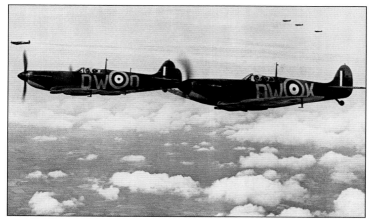

Spitfires in the air during the Battle of Britain

Doris Lilley agreed. "My brother was injured in North Africa in 1941. Wars are awful. But we must remember the brave men and women who fought to keep Britain free in the Second World War, and in wars since then. They are all heroes."

George's wife, Violet, and her school friends, Helen Probert and Margaret Naker, were also at the reunion. The women were at school together in 1940 in Sussex, where they witnessed several battles in the air.

The meeting was organized by Zoe and Zak, the Buckden grandchildren.

"We became interested in the Battle of Britain when Grandpa found his old RAF locker," said Zak. "Grandma and Grandpa had lots of memories of the war."

"And we realized how lucky we are that they survived," added Zoe. "We wanted to do something special for them."

Everyone at today's reunion agreed that it was a very special occasion indeed.

WORLD WAR II OVERVIEW

THE HOLOCAUST
The German leader, Adolf Hitler, and his Nazi party were deeply prejudiced against Jews and other groups of people. The Nazis sent these "undesirables" to concentration (prison) camps where the prisoners were starved, tortured, and many killed, including about 6 million Jews.

RUSSIA AND THE USA JOIN THE ALLIES
In June 1941, Russia joined the Allies after Germany broke their agreement and invaded. Then, in December 1941, the USA also declared war after Japan attacked the US navy base at Pearl Harbor in Hawaii.

THE WAR IN THE PACIFIC
Japan invaded China, countries in Southeast Asia, and islands in the Pacific Ocean. In 1944, Japanese kamikaze pilots started flying suicide missions to bomb Allied warships. The war in the Pacific resulted in heavy casualties on both sides.

D-DAY (DELIVERANCE DAY)

In June 1944, more than 150,000 British, American, and Canadian soldiers secretly sailed across the English Channel to invade German-occupied France and take it back for the Allies. After a bitter struggle, the Germans started to retreat.

VE DAY (VICTORY IN EUROPE)

On May 8th, 1945, Germany finally surrendered and the Allies celebrated VE Day.

ATOMIC BOMBS

By August 1945, Japan was still refusing to surrender. The Allies, led by the USA, dropped atomic bombs on two Japanese cities. These bombs, the most powerful ever made, killed more than 200,000 people and caused long-term illnesses to civilians. After six long years, the war was finally over.

THE UNITED NATIONS

In an effort to prevent the horrors of such a war from happening again, countries around the globe formed the United Nations in October 1945.

Remembering

War memorials help us to remember those who died, while encouraging us to hope for a peaceful future.

OUR WALL

Here inscribed the names of friends we knew
Young men with whom we often flew,
Scrambled to many angels high,
They knew that they or friends might die.
Many were very scarcely trained,
And many badly burnt or maimed.
Behind each name a story lies
Of bravery in summer skies;
Though many brave unwritten tales
Were simply told in vapour trails.
Many now lie in sacred graves
And many rest beneath the waves.
Outnumbered every day they flew,
Remembered here as just 'The Few'.

William L B Walker
616 Squadron

This poem was written by RAF Flight Lieutenant
William Walker, who was a Spitfire pilot during
the Battle of Britain. It can be seen at the National
Memorial to the Few in Kent, England.

Battle in the Air Quiz

See if you can remember the answers to these questions about what you have read.

1. In what year was the Battle of Britain fought?

2. What do the letters RAF stand for?

3. What was Grandpa's RAF base called and what was his squadron number?

4. What type of aircraft did Grandpa fly in the Battle of Britain?

5. What did Grandma sometimes see outside her classroom window?

6. In World War II, the fighting nations were divided into two opposing groups. What were they called?

7. All together, about how many people died in World War II?

8.   Which country did Panesar Singh come from?

9.   Which character in the book met King George VI and why?

10.   What did the rationing of food ensure?

11.   What does ARP stand for?

12.   What kind of animal did the pupils at Oxmore Girls School raise in the schoolyard?

13.   What did the Women's Land Army do?

14.   Why did Grandpa particularly thank Panesar Singh at the reunion?

15.   What was VE Day?

Answers on page 125.

Glossary

Ack ack gun
Nickname for an anti-aircraft gun used to shoot at enemy aircraft.

Air raid
A bomb attack from the air.

ARP (Air Raid Precautions)
Instructions to follow in case of an air raid.

Chamberlain, Neville
British Prime Minister, 1937–40. He declared war on Germany in 1939.

Churchill, Winston
British Prime Minister, 1940–45 (and 1951–55). He led Britain during most of World War II.

Dispersal
Location of aircraft spaced out around the airfield so they're not a target.

Evacuate
Move away from a dangerous place.

Gas mask
A breathing device worn to cover the nose, mouth, and eyes to give protection from a gas attack.

Hitler, Adolf
German dictator, 1933–45. His invasion of Poland started World War II. He is known for masterminding the Holocaust.

Holocaust
In World War II, the mass murder of millions of Jews and others by Adolf Hitler and the Nazis.

Invade
Enter a place, such as a country, with the aim of taking control of it.

Luftwaffe
German air force.

RAF (Royal Air Force)
British air force.

Rationing
Limiting food and other goods during shortages so that everyone has a fair share.

Refugee
Someone forced to leave their country to find safety.

Scramble
Rapid takeoff of fighter aircraft.

Squadron
A military unit.

Answers to the Battle in the Air Quiz:
1. 1940; **2.** Royal Air Force; **3.** RAF Lyddenstone, No.606 Squadron; **4.** Spitfire; **5.** Aircraft fighting in the sky; **6.** Allies and Axis; **7.** 60 million; **8.** India; **9.** Doris Lilley, because she had shot down a German bomber; **10.** There was enough food for everyone; **11.** Air Raid Precautions; **12.** Pigs; **13.** Helped to grow much-needed food while farmers were at war; **14.** Panesar Singh had saved his life during the Battle of Britain; **15.** Victory in Europe Day on May 8th, 1945, when Germany finally surrendered.

Index